WHET

W H E T

POEMS
by Michael Chitwood

OHIO REVIEW BOOKS • ATHENS, OHIO

FOR JACOB, STILL TO WRESTLE HIS ANGEL

CONTENTS

ONE

This Thrilling Dirt

- 3   Concrete World
- 4   This Is the Day the Lord Has Made
- 5   What We Can Ill Afford
- 6   Pilgrim's Progress
- 7   Looking for Horace Kephart's Grave, Bryson City, NC
- 8   Opossum Burn
- 9   Church Piano
- 11   Moving the Piano
- 12   Woods Piano
- 13   General Delivery
- 14   Shotguns
- 15   Fossil
- 16   Photograph of Five Men Crossing a Creek
- 17   Blue Smoke

TWO

Following A Path Made By Water

- 21   By Water, Again
- 22   What Day Is This?
- 23   Looking for Blues
- 24   The Buoys
- 25   You Can Observe a Lot Just by Watching
- 26   The Rain's Ability to Open the Doors of Perception, Exposing the Dual Nature of Existence
- 27   After the Missionaries
- 28   Daddy X
- 30   Proof of the Existence of God
- 31   Following a Path Made by Water

THREE

The Law's Blue Light

    35 Logic
    36 Whet
    37 Sleepless
    38 The Quick
    39 Who Knows?

FOUR

Getting It Straight And Narrow

    43 An Explanation of Nine-thirty
    44 Bibles
    45 The Cost of Being Metaphor
    46 Saints in the Aisles of Route 40 Gro. and Feed
    47 The Delivery
    48 You Must Come in at the Door
    49 The Truth
    51 White
    52 Getting It Straight and Narrow
    55 An Explanation of Six-thirty

Books by Michael Chitwood:

Whet
Salt Works
Martyrdom of the Onions

Copyright © 1995 Michael Chitwood
All rights reserved

Design: Joyce Barlow Dodd
Composition: Sans Serif
(set in Bembo; display headings in Delphian)
Printed at Thomson-Shore

Library of Congress Cataloging in Publication Data
Chitwood, Michael
    Whet : poems / Michael Chitwood.
      p.   cm.
    ISBN 0–942148–16–9 (pbk.)
    I. Title.
PS3553.H535W48   1995
811'.54—dc20   95–17686
                                                      CIP

(An Ohio Review Book)

ONE

This Thrilling Dirt

Concrete World

    Welcome Concrete World,
    where prepositions are unnecessary.
    Welcome concrete dogs, frogs, owls, mushrooms, little boys peeing,
        little boys fishing the gravel lot from concrete benches, ducks,
        chickens, deer kneeling, deer standing, miniature love seats,
        empty and occupied.
    Welcome flowerpots, birdbaths and their pedestals, gutter shunts and
        parking lot bumpers, all things ornamental and useful.
    Welcome St. Francis and your concrete chickadees.
    Welcome little Mothers of Christ, little Marys, marching in a line
        like concrete majorettes.
    Welcome elves, gnomes, unicorns, phoenix, brownies, spirits, sprites,
        even the risen Lord, all made concrete.
    Souvenirs and Gifts. Welcome. Welcome.

This Is the Day the Lord Has Made

"I'll have no truck with angels,"
he says to his stunned boots,
sole-up by the silage cutter.
The snapped drive chain writhes
in the dust of his field.
His ring finger wears his ring
and one rusted link of the chain.
"No truck," he says into his chest pocket.
His watch pays no heed.
The dust gets up and does a jig.
His lonesome finger scratches an itch.
He thinks he'll just lay back a little.
A cross hangs on a thermal, a hawk
hauling its keen hunger into heaven.

What We Can Ill Afford

Desire is the invalid mother of the mayor,
camped out on the front porch,
lording it over Main Street.
Her hungry eyes know
who's been in town with a new dress on.
Lax Pugh has banked a season's tobacco
and kept a little money to burn in this pocket.
His thirst is tugging him toward the Circle Lunch
and she knows.
She's not going anywhere.
She'll be there when the red neon O
pinks the asphalt,
when the oldest one comes to fetch him.
She rings her little bell for the help.
Everyone comes to town needing something.
She means to see if they get it.

Pilgrim's Progress

It used to say "happy motoring,"
all lower case in jaunty slant lettering,
some ad man's Wednesday afternoon solution
to the problem of slumping gas sales.
I've come down NC 87
by the antique white sprays of dogwood,
the purple splashes of redbud,
the creeks brown and swollen,
the ground so sodden it can hold no more
and have stopped as the sign instructed
to see sprung card tables
littered with outgrown and outcast clothes,
chipped depression glass, scorched pots,
whatnots and knick-knacks and gimcracks,
every worthless item from someone's life,
displayed in front on the empty garage bays.
The pump islands are cracked and weedy.
A huge woman in red knit pants waves
and above her, like an idea,
only the word "happy."

Looking for Horace Kephart's Grave, Bryson City, NC

I don't think he's up here
in the oak-filtered light
and grease fumes from the Hardee's
down on Spring Street.
He's slipped off again
into the blue haze over Deep Creek.
There's no one here to name that knob
off to the left
or to say what creek is flashing
its silver change
behind the Jackson Savings Bank.
There's just the squirrel
working a pine cone on a Quiett's stone
and the roots
tipping the carved markers with their slow crawl.

Opossum Burn

Because the opossum is wise,
it is killed foolishly.
It contemplates as it walks,
which is the way
it came to this country,
grandsires so lost in thought
they did not see the mother continent
setting sail like a pleasure ship
for another hemisphere.

They are Arab in their thinking,
musing on the numeral zero,
the hunger number, wide mouth,
empty inside. They gnaw that thought
and do not see the Caprice bearing down.

This one rolled to the shoulder.
Two weeks it has ascended.
Soon only an oval scald in the weeds
will hold its place on earth.

Church Piano

Like an invalid
it took up the corner.

Banished from heaven
by the electric lutes

and oboe
of the organ,

it went out
of tune

at the empty
hands of children.

Children loved
the grin

under the dark,
hinged lip.

They would lift
and bang

their tuneless jubilee.
Bring me your quick,

it sang.
The game was

who could play
and snatch

their hands back
before the fall

of the lid.
"Children, children,"

it called,
"bring me your fingers."

Moving the Piano

Like a shut-in
it stalls at the door.

We knock tunes,
nudge it out.

It balks
on the ramp,

slaughter-bound bull.
It odds the truck bed.

Bumps and curves
begin a song

and leave off.
Its small feet

screech the sheet metal.
Nervous, it shifts

the load,
pulls on the engine.

Hard black hide,
its heart drums hymns.

Convenience shoppers stop,
lift up their eyes.

It rides,
tiny hooves and song.

Woods Piano

    Gravels ping
    the running boards.

    We drag dust
    and odd notes.

    Sprung upright,
    gone in tune.

    Quick, the ramp.
    It slides

    and tries a gospel
    number but quiets.

    Clorox bottles, box springs,
    a brethren Maytag,

    but here it will chief
    and wild.

    The rain will eat
    its wired heart

    for the hymns
    and hammer beats.

General Delivery

What they had to say
they kept to themselves.

He polished a shoe
like someone wishing for a genie.

She picked up salt
with two fingers and a thumb.

That was all she needed.
He did the other shoe.

His tie hung all week
with its knot.

Sunday he put it on.
Sunday her feet hurt.

Either one could knock
on the fuel tank

and know how long
the heat would last.

Shotguns

They leaned
in their room,
a gang like uncles
before Thanksgiving dinner.
Mother,
coming from the bedroom,
would catch my fingers
on the glass.

"Hold your breath and squeeze,"
he whispered,
handing me the awkward weight
of the 12 gauge.
The squirrel worked a pine cone.
The shell nestled in its oiled chamber.
He put his arms around me,
and his kindness
bruised my shoulder.

Fossil

A toe bone,
you think because you're on your daily walk,
the toe bone connected to the foot,
the leg, the hip, the smooth stairs
of the spine and then you're climbing
the little mound of the cerebellum.
What a view. Never mind
your aching feet.
Of course, it could be a piece of chalk
or maybe the entire skeleton
of a small reptile.
A thumb bone,
you think when it's in your hand.
With applied mathematics,
it's simple to rebuild an animal
from any of its digits
as long as you know the bone
for what it is,
the body's pennywhistle.
Put it to your lips.
Both larks and children will answer.

Photograph of Five Men Crossing a Creek

Any wishful thought
from a hunting or woodcutting companion
would bring his famous quip:
"And people in Hell want ice water."

It's scrawled
like sticks dropped in snow
on the back of this photograph,
a vengeful caption.

Of a hard, silent mountain people,
he was the hardest,
coldly quiet as a winter night.

Here, he goes across,
shoulder high on four brethren.
Where he's going,
it's too rough for a Model T.

I can't help but notice
how, even with his awkward box,
the others pick through the stream,
babystepping to foot-sized stones.
The water is quick with melt-off.

Blue Smoke

Singing like a hornet,
a 125 or maybe 250
buzzes on the other side of the pines.

Somebody's teenager
is burning oil, the blue smoke in puffs
from the tailpipe.
He's working his wrist
to throttle anger or lust
or he doesn't know what
into wheelies and crossups.

The knobbies spew mud
that taps him on the shoulder.
He won't look back.
All that's important is ahead
in the tire ruts and washboard ripples,
all that counts is taking the curve,
leaning into it
and riding the lift,
splattered as he is with this place,
this thrilling dirt.

TWO

Following a Path Made by Water

By Water, Again

Dusk, the hemlock clatters.

*

Pellets tick against the window,
against the glass of the sidewalk,
every step at risk.

*

The nights' bones crack.
Music drains from the radio,
and all the outside dark
comes in.

*

The clock's hands are frozen.
This minute, the next, the same.
Only ice ticks.

*

Overhead, the maple scratches
like a cat lonely for company.
It wants in.

*

Our little light sputters,
drowns in its own melting.
Our listening patrols the dark.

*

Saws gnaw at dawn.
Every standing tree is in prayer.
Everybody is looking up, pointing.

What Day Is This?

May, our little name for the patch of timothy
under cicada churr and jay scream.
Is a month real as a pasture?
When you come back from its new grass
are your shoes darkened with dew?

The dogwoods are in a funk.
They've shredded their love letters
and are dropping the pieces individually,
falling out of love one word at a time.
A cardinal pushes notes like tacks
into the spongy blue board of today's sky.
The map the dew made
is fading out of the leather.

I've got time on my hands,
the smudge of the morning news.
The cardinal is back, a red pock
in the sweet gum.
May's engines are overheating,
the oil scorching, smoking blue.
If you go out to the pond,
May will be there too, getting loud,
getting a little rough in its language.

Looking for Blues

This is no metaphor,
the poles, strapped to the jeep front, whip,
knobby tires churn the sand,
vacation shadows the faces of the men.
They have two days.
This is about fish,
not music or the chemicals schooling in our bodies
making us want to quit our jobs,
making us want to buy a big car
or get in trouble with a woman
who lets her skirt ride when she sits down
and tilts her head back to blow the blue smoke
of her I-don't-give-a-damn at the ceiling.
This is not about fatback biscuit music.
It's about a gullet with fins,
a rocketing hunger these men are looking for.
Once they're running, you can hook them with
blown fuses, pig skins, beer bottle caps,
any glint or snatch of stink.
Once they've gone this far
anything is like anything else.

The Buoys

Again tonight,
they are restless.

"Dock," "God,"
"Dim Tank,"

they talk
on water.

The dead,
I think,

pull those bell
ropes, the salt

rosaries, the worry
of the underworld.

Their tongues rust,
lock at the root.

Acetylene
and tonnage

is the balm
I give.

Deep to deep,
their tone,

they wear
they warn.

You Can Observe a Lot Just by Watching

If dogs wrote novels,
the subtext would be the yellow,
tan, and pale pink puffs of scent
one finds unexpectedly,
mouth-watering and hair-raising.

If snakes wrote novels,
metaphor would dart into the sentences,
tongue out, tang of rat sweat,
sweet and sour of the grasshopper's tobacco juice.

The plot whines like quarrelsome children.
You know the story,
something happens, then something else,
oblivious to the sequins of fireflies
on dusk's dress,
the silver lamé of rain on the lake,
mockingbirds splashing like bluegill in the drenched foliage,
the pock where a bass snatched a May fly,
the growing exclamation,
O, O, O, O.

*The Rain's Ability to Open the Doors of Perception,
Exposing the Dual Nature of Existence*

In the Hot Line at the Stop-N-Go
I realize the drizzle

has silvered the backs
of the Smoking Section's windows

and made it possible for me to be
myself and see myself a spirit

in the slick, black street outside.
Now I stab the stained wand

into the mustard pot of two worlds
and reflect on the wonder

of dressing a sausage dog both
within the incense of diced onions

and the slash of traffic on Airport Road.
Praise be to hot chili.

Dog and change in hand,
I wait at the exit for an entrance.

After the Missionaries

We walk on lava,
solid of a liquid rock.

God is our rock.
Rocks were gods.

I say I am saved
but row far out,

too far to walk
even if they could

and say "Water,
I still believe in you."

Daddy X

The beagle yelps along the hot scent,
a path a body has made.
She strings barks, self-contained pearls,
on the invisible cord of aroma.

"It's worth putting up with the shit,"
says X, who these days is only drinking a little beer
in the evenings.
He motions to the turds
that almost look like they've been placed
around the concrete patio.
There's one just beside the artificial turf mat
that says WELCOME,
the white capitals splotched with the muddy rosettes
left by beagle paws.

"I love to hear them work," says X,
his real given name
that for 20 years he did his best to live up to.
When the scent is hot
the little bitch takes it up an octave,
excited, or sounding like excitement
the way anger can sometimes sound
like the breathy whispers of passion.

X's house is in the bottom
of this natural bowl
and he is the faithful audience
of the honeysuckle theater,
the dog's knowing what to do
even without training.

They go out on their own
when they feel the need.

"I rarely see it," he says
of what goes through the brush
leaving a live path

that causes the dogs to shout
in their language to him listening in his.

His son's forgiven him,
brings the grandchildren by
to hear the races
and walk down to the pond
where Daddy X feeds the catfish.
It's pure X
the way he's set it up,
banging the tin cup on the dock
so they school up from the bottom
and roil
while he calls, "kitty, kitty, kitty,"
and the kids love it.

Proof of the Existence of God

It rained in the night.
It rained in the window,
an open window.
The night was open
because we had nothing
written in its tiny window on the calendar.
So it rained in an open night.

It is the power, the mover,
the repellent in tag.
From one who is it,
the others scatter.
It holds the scatter
and the rain's opening.
The night is a gauge
to be rained in.
It did the raining,
the much needed rain
or the cursed rain,
the ground holding all it can,
a handkerchief full from weeping.
"That's not it,"
says the weeping man.
"Just forget it,"
but he goes on weeping.

It goes on raining
and the nights open
like God or a window,
that specific vagueness
where it is,
where you are it
and the rain is the rain.

Following a Path Made by Water

I love the biting, blood-hungry flies.
They make me wave my arms around my ears.
In the field I must look like I'm dancing.
Sometimes I catch one against my cheek
and smear his packet of thrivings there.
I honor him by wearing his paint
to make ready.
I've walked by the mud, spangled with bottleflies.
I've walked by the crayfish, with his one arm raised,
his one question.
I've walked by the witch doctor, his scuffling wings
and here is the way water went.
The long grass is pushed down.
It was held under. I follow,
deeper into the pasture.

THREE

The Law's Blue Light

Logic

Carol's uncle raises pigs and chickens.

On a trip to the farm, Carol
sees 48 legs and 33 heads.

How many times does Carol have to be told
that chickens walk perfectly well
without their heads?

"You can get hungry full of sympathy,"
her uncle tells her.
"Do you think those hogs
would turn *you* down?
They know how to fill a belly,
theirs or yours."

The fly on the sidemeat
crosses his legs.

Solve for x.

Whet

And then I see the film snaking
through the projector in elementary school,

the proud girl who knew how to thread the thing
even when the teacher didn't or said he didn't so he could

reach under her thin arms to help the teeth
find the edges they were looking for.

The room goes dark, and the king cobra falls
for the flute music curling past the stops.

Then the king is eating a lesser snake
and though I know the eaten one

will bunch and be digested
I keep getting it wrong, seeing

the swallowed snake feeding down the length
of the cobra until they are

some ancient picture of the world,
one full length inside the other

and when the king crawls, the eaten
crawls backward out of Eden, maybe.

The girl is on a tall stool behind the projector,
like a queen. She lets the film

glide on her hand. It slinks for her,
and she sucks hard candy, hones it to a razor.

Sleepless

The musk of something wanting to be
sets up a clamour in the neighborhood.
Mrs. Pettibone has locked her dachshund bitch
in the garage and now dogs for miles
have developed an interest
in the fit of key and lock slot.
The distant moon is unmoved but anoints
the scene just the same with a cool lotion.
Conner has wrapped his chain around the slender
hybrid dogwood. He saws, his ardor expensive.
His master begs for quiet, but the breeze
keeps unleashing.

The Quick

    The chemist from Building 9 takes a smoke break on the concrete step outside the lab. He knows better.

    He knows he sips his own death through the little straw filled with fine Virginia gold leaf.

    He cannot tell you why. He can tell you why the smoke works. A ghost streams in the branches of his lungs; his blood has come to love it.

    There have been several days of rain. He notices that the ground *ticks* as it sogs. It is trying to take in the standing water. Flagstones, he thinks. A path of flagstones.

    Laid end to end, with synaptic spaces between, our odd-shaped loves—tobacco, basketball, our own boyhood, lilac water—make a path out of the yard. It's the implied fit, like long-separated continents, that allows you to step over the sob-swollen ground.

    You can know either velocity, which is the love affair between speed and direction, or exact location, according to the Heisenberg Uncertainty Principle. Not both. The quick or the dead.

    The boy is careful of the mud between the stones. He hitches his stride. His shoes are white. A hummingbird sips from a chalice of trumpet creeper near the stone he turns on. He shouts to the screen door, "Aren't you coming?" When he left the house she was pulling on a Sunday shoe with one finger. She wore the dress he loved to see on the line, the way it wore the wind.

Who Knows?

Desire is threatening Reason again.
The music's been loud for an hour
and between tracks
you can hear chairs scraping,
doors slamming.
It could be over a pork chop or new dress,
who knows?
Somebody's probably already called the law.
Soon the blue lights will run wild
by the lawn chairs and birdbath.

FOUR

Getting It Straight and Narrow

An Explanation of Nine-thirty

I'm in the backyard,
the twin engines and prop-jets from the local airport
trolling for me,
letting down the growling nets I slip through.
the morning is climbing past,
leaving its vapor trail to unravel like loose yarn.

The mockingbird has started his Friday lecture,
a little late but without written text.
Some Amish fasten their coats with straight pins
because they believe buttons too worldly.

The mockingbird digresses.
He is here and now, and I am,
afloat in the backyard.
On a Pennsylvania state route,
there's a black buggy, a black horse pulling
and the mown hay and fence posts and locust grind
rock in its wake.

Bibles

Preachers raise them like hatchets,
shake them at us, make threats
and follow us home to lunch.
My father's deluxe
has its own tongue, the satin
bound-in bookmark, forked, always out.
At the Day's Rest, a certain woman smooths
her rumpled blouse with the donated spine.
At Eldercare, the loud one smacks his palm
with the edge of the green pocket-size.
He's forgotten he's given up cigarettes.
Alone in the formal living room,
the New Testament text
of the special edition
breaks out in red welts
every time the Son of God speaks.

The Cost of Being Metaphor

> "Lazarus, come out."
> —John 11.43

The numbness never left
his left hand.
He'd lain on it wrong
in his four-day brush with death
and now it remained asleep,
so he began to use it for miracles
of his own,
fishing potatoes from boiling water,
pouring oil into the palm
and igniting it, his own hand a lamp.
At night, you could see its ghostly floating
through his house.
He was too odd.
All he wanted to talk about was his comeback.
Had you seen it?
When did you hear?
What were you doing when you heard?
He became only that moment
with its whiff of the raised body.

Saints in the Aisles of Route 40 Gro. and Feed

St. Augustine has asked to see the Night Train,
                                            or Thunderbird,
one of the fortified wines,
just for old time's sake.

St. Paul is looking for a salve, Udder Balm
or Neet's Foot Oil
                to draw off hot blood.

St. Theresa pays for baler twine
                          and a packet of Feen-A-Mint
with change from a Mason jar.

St. Francis finds the Calf Starter
and pigs' feet
          he's been looking for.

St. Sebastian wants to know
                  if the tomato stakes are in.

St. Thomas Aquinas says the Almanac was wrong
about the March snow,
                  both in accumulation and frequency.

Why are you surprised?
Don't you know the gospel
                  is just across the road
in the ditch trash and rabbit tobacco?

The Delivery

It's the way you wake up once or twice in your life
if you're lucky:

The snake came up on the porch like an insurance man,
uninvited and making himself at home,
and most everyone suddenly remembered something they'd left inside.

So that our grandmother might sleep again
this side of Paradise,
we took a hoe to the harmless thing
and then noticed the huge bulge and decided to see
what its last supper consisted of.

The pocketknife unzipped it
and a squirrel-sized rat rolled out, hit the hard ground
and woke to terror,
fur wet with its own dying.

It screamed and shit and shot for cover,
born, as they say, again.

You Must Come in at the Door

It turns the tin pie plate
on its string in the garden.
The crows in their black jumpsuits
scatter from its racket.

It worries the sycamore,
the big hands busy themselves,
green back and white palm,
what next, what next?

So wide,
it raises the nap on a field of rye.
So low,
it turns the mica-spangled dust.

Its hand is on the sparrow.
It breathes life into fire
and purges the forest floor.

It will throw the road into your eyes
and leave the precinct.
Around the corner, it whistles a hymn.
It has no stop.

The Truth

The Whole Truth

What do you have to say for yourself?
The wind, for instance, flips through some flashcards
of intransitive verbs.
The whole oak nods,
the big dumb brute,
doesn't he know what this means,
doesn't he know what I'm saying?
The shutter knocks but will not come in.
Let no one wonder.
The wind will wear
whatever hat it chooses
and go down the street whistling.

The Simple Truth

The simple truth is the sooty flue
and its blistered fuel tanks,
squatting out back in their nests of weeds.
The simple truth is the screen door
pulled to its slap by a slack, rusty spring.
The simple truth is you miss the feedback
coming through the PA in the square
"Today. . . today. . . I declare myself. . . myself."
Admit it. Our lives are on the lam
from better lives, the palaces, the peacocks
in the garden, the tsar
with his silver ice tongs.
The simple truth is we wish it had been otherwise.

The Sad Truth

The sad truth is the one shoe

you see beside interstates.
Where is the other shoe?
Why did it leave us here?
The sad truth is they identified everyone
by what they were wearing,
but the impact had hung someone's coat
in a bare oak.
It was out on a limb
not far from the ground
as if he'd taken it off
to keep it from getting soiled while he napped.

White

Thrown down
on the stink and slop,
it sweetens the feed lot.

Jut, like Confederate stones,
teeth in the red clay bank
of an infant's gums.

Cells the sky sluffs off,
it piles.
It closes the interstate.

Fish belly of the leaves
before a storm.
It shakes.

Gospel, rolled back.
The snapped blank belief.
The blind look.

Getting It Straight and Narrow

Crayola and pot glue.
Joseph and Mary scissored

from the Big Book
of Old Testament Heroes.

We stab a gold clasp
into their hearts

and open its wings
to fasten them to the page.

Careful, the teacher says,
as one point enters the quick

under my right thumb nail.
I know that I live.

The sweet red Kool-Aid
stains our tongues.

*

Emanuel, Wonderful Counselor,
King of Kings,

Good Shepherd, Son of
God, Son of

Man, He that Comes After,
Prince of Peace,

"Jesus H. Christ,"
my uncle said,

watching his sock
soak with blood.

*

I've got the piece
of pie

not withstanding
down in my heart.

*

Howard, Harlan, Henry?
My book bag bumped my back.

Horatio, no, no.
The dust of the road,

Hallelujah, maybe,
danced in tiny hurricanes.

Hope, nope.
That's a girl.

Hank, yea, Hank.
Jesus Hank Christ.

Nice guy,
works at the mill.

*

Handle like a tongue depressor
stapled to big flaps of cardboard.

Jesus on one side,
handsome, Rock Hudson with a beard.

The ad for Lynch's
Funeral Home on the other.

Jesus/Rock looked longingly
at a cloud-smeared sky.

Lynch's promised to be
my comfort in time of need.

One side, then the other
fanning the flames

of brimstone the preacher
was conjuring up.

              *

Lucky Strikes, daily bacon, white socks.
Watch in his bib's chest pocket stopped.

His coat and hat hung on the hook
for the last time.

"The Lord wanted him home,"
but so did I,

and that was the departure,
the long leaving town.

Even his old Ford gave up
and they used the skeleton

of my swing set
to hoist the blown block.

There it is, black heart,
rain dark, hoses dangling.

What the matter was
is still there, inside.

An Explanation of Six-thirty

The sun in slats through the fence.
Is it the shadow on the fescue
or the planks of light
that mark this time of day's momentary stall?
I go back and forth.

Perception is the threshold we cross
to cross the next threshold,
the ladder with one rung.
We love its delicious pressure on our instep
and must step off.

The beaten lamé is mitered by afternoon's end.
I will unlatch the gate and shade my eyes.
My shadow will have to make its own way
past the fence's stabs and blinks.

photo by Jimmy W. Crawford

Michael Chitwood is the author of *Salt Works* and *Martyrdom of the Onions*. Born in the shadows of the Virginia Blue Ridge, he now lives in Chapel Hill, North Carolina.

ACKNOWLEDGEMENTS

Grateful acknowledgement is made to the following journals, in which the poems listed first appeared, sometimes in slightly different form:

Appalachian Heritage (General Delivery)
Berkeley Poetry Review (Pilgrim's Progress)
Fine Madness (Moving the Piano; Woods Piano; Following a Path Made by Water; The Cost of Being Metaphor; The Delivery)
Georgia Journal (Shotguns)
Massachusetts Review (An Explanation of 9:30, An Explanation of 6:30)
The Ohio Review (By Water, Again; The Truth)
Poetry (What Day Is This?; Church Piano; After the Missionaries; Who Knows?)
Poetry East (Saints in the Aisles of the Route 40 Gro. and Feed)
Prairie Schooner (The Quick)
Shenandoah (Fossil)
Southern Review (Photograph of Five Men Crossing a Creek)
Sow's Ear (Logic)
Threepenny Review (Looking for Blues; The Buoys; The Rain's Ability to Open the Doors of Perception, Exposing the Dual Nature of Existence; Whet)
Turning Dances (White)

"This Is the Day the Lord Has Made" first appeared in *The Odd Angles of Heaven*, David Craig and Janet McCann, editors, Harold Shaw Publishers. "The Buoys," "Following a Path Made by Water," and "Looking for Blues" were reprinted in *Water, An Outer Banks Anthology*, Coquina Press.

Thanks to the Richard H. Thornton Endowment of Lynchburg College for giving me the time to write some of these poems; praise to Al Maginnes, Michael McFee, Georgann Eubanks, Maggi Grace, Bill Newton, and Tom Andrews, who always help; thanks to Bob Kinsley and Joyce Barlow Dodd for their work in the salt mine; wild gratitude to Wayne Dodd for sending me back to the whet rock; and for all, thanks to Jean.